# ABORTIONS

# IN THE CHURCH

# ABORTIONS IN THE CHURCH

## Divine Strategies to Spiritual Deliverance

Author Derashay Zorn

Copyright © 2017 by D.O.R.M. International Publishing

All rights reserved. Except as permitted under the U.S. Copyright Act of 1976, no part of this publication may be reproduced, distributed, or transmitted in any form or by any mean, or stored in a database or retrieval system, without the prior written permission of the publisher. Permission request must be approved in writing by D.O.R.M. International Publishing by emailing request to **permission@divine-order.org**

All scripture quotations, unless otherwise indicated, are taken from the HOLY BIBLE, NEW INTERNATIONAL VERSION®. NIV®. Copyright © 1973, 1978, 1984 by International Bible Society. Used by permission of Zondervan. All rights reserved.

"Scripture quotations are from The Holy Bible, English Standard Version", copyright © 2001 by Crossway Bibles, a publishing ministry of Good News Publishers. Used by permission. All rights reserved."

For information about special discounts for bulk purchase, contact the sales department at **sales@inthechurch.com**

Designed by D' Technology

D.O.R.M. International Publishing
Visit our website at **www.divine-order.org**
Printed in the United State of America
First Edition: February 2017
10 9 8 7 6 5 4 3 2 1
Library of Congress Cataloging-in-Publication Data
Derashay Worthen-Zorn
Abortions in The Church-Divine Strategies to Spiritual Deliverance/
Derashay Worthen-Zorn – 1st ed.
ISBN-13: 978-0986249303
ISBN-10: 0986249300

I dedicate this book to Divine Order Restoration Ministries International family, friends, partners, and associates. In addition, to all those who are willing and ready to overcome any opposition and give birth to their purpose, dreams, vision, desire, etc. These words of wisdom will guide you in overcoming everything that has hindered you from giving birth to God's word for your life.

# Table of Content

- ACKNOWLEDGEMENTS .................................................................. 1
- INTRODUCTION ............................................................................ 3

## SPIRITUAL CONCEPTION ............................................................. 7
- Process of Spiritual Conceptions ................................................. 8

## SPIRITUAL MISCARRIAGE ........................................................... 11
- What is a Spiritual Miscarriage? ................................................ 12
- What Causes a Spiritual Miscarriage? ........................................ 12
- Identifying Spiritual Miscarriages High-Risk Factors ................ 13
- Signs of a Spiritual Miscarriage ................................................. 16
- Spiritual Miscarriage Prevention Methods ................................ 25
- Exercise: ..................................................................................... 29

## SPIRITUAL ABORTION ................................................................ 37
- What is a Spiritual Abortion? ..................................................... 38
- What causes Spiritual Abortions? .............................................. 38
- Identifying Spiritual Abortions High-Risk Factors .................... 40
- Warning Signs of Spiritual Abortions ........................................ 43
- Spiritual Abortion Prevention Methods .................................... 51
- Exercise ...................................................................................... 55

## SPIRITUAL STILLBORN ............................................................... 63
- What is a Spiritual Stillborn? ..................................................... 64
- What causes a Spiritual Stillborn? ............................................. 64
- Identifying Spiritual Stillborn High-Risk Factors ...................... 65
- Spiritual Stillborn Warning Signs .............................................. 68
- Prevention Methods for Spiritual Stillbirths ............................. 77
- Exercise ...................................................................................... 80

## WORK BOOK SAMPLE ................................................................ 88

## Acknowledgements

I want to first give honor and thanks to God for trusting me with this book and every project associated with it. It has been such an honor to scribe for you.

I would like to express my sincere gratitude to my husband, Eric Zorn, who gave me the support and time needed to complete this project. You have been instrumental in assisting me in delivering this book. Thanks a million. I give thanks and honor to my young men Eric, D'Eric and Ericson for your love and support through this endeavor.

I would like to thank Denise Walker, founder and chief editor of Armor of Hope Writing Services, for your commitment to making this project shine with a spirit of excellence. I give thanks to Destiny Nixon for your feedback and all my family and friends contributions. I would also like to thank every individual who purchases this book. You are bringing it to life.

Special thanks to my Pastor, Dr. Leland L. Jones, of Greater New Light Missionary Baptist Church for being an excellent and supportive leader. Thank you for being instrumental in my walk and keeping me from falling into the pitfalls of having a spiritual miscarriage, abortion, or stillborn as it concerns my purpose in the Lord. Thanks for the push, motivation, and encouragement. It has been very instrumental on this journey. You truly have a shepherd's heart.

## Introduction

In a world where Christians are against the murder of a life, it could be found very strange that when it comes to spiritual murders, we become very silent. Christians are very radical and vocal when it comes to abortion protests, rallies or discussions. I often wonder if there will ever be a time when we are just as radical and vocal about spiritual abortions. If there was ever a time to become very vocal are radical about spiritual deaths and murders, I would say the time is now. Natural deaths and murders are taking place at an alarming rate, and it is just a snapshot of what's happening spiritually in the lives of Gods children. To reduce and eliminate the bloodshed that we are seeing across this world, we must start with the elimination of what's taking place spiritually within mankind. Murder and deaths within the church are happening by way of spiritual abortions, miscarriages, and stillbirths. It is time to build healthy churches that are conducive to conceive, carry, and deliver the promises and purpose of God within their lives, no longer putting to death visions, dreams, goals, aspirations, and desires.

However, there cannot be a delivery until there is a deliverance.

# ABORTIONS IN THE CHURCH

# 1

# Spiritual Conception

## Process of Spiritual Conceptions

Spiritual conception is known as the inception of spiritual pregnancy. It is the moment in time where the word of God is released in the life of an individual. If the word of God is not released, then no conception can come forth. Where there is no conception, there are no pregnancies, there are no births, and there is no fulfillment of purpose. It's important to have a mutual intimate relationship with God so that you can hear and know of the great things that He has planned for your life. God will also send His servants to confirm His plan of purpose into your life as well. If we don't have an ear for the spirit of God, then how will we obtain our purpose or know which way we should go. The word of God is what directs us, guides us, leads us, trains us and impregnates us with purpose. When the word is officially released, we have the choice to have a spiritual miscarriage, abortion, stillborn or continue with the pregnancy. This book will address spiritual miscarriage, abortion, and stillborn that are taking place in the body of Christ as individuals fail to move in their purpose. . The sequel will address spiritual birthing.

The ability to carry the pregnancy of dreams, visions, desires, aspirations is not completed when the word is conceived, it must take root through a process called implementation.

A word that does not take root when it is conceived positions an individual to be at high risk for having a spiritual miscarriage, abortion or stillborn with that word. When a word is conceived, the implementation must begin with the individual.

Implantation is the process in which the word goes through to become attached (take root) so, then it can become embedded (roots grow) within the individual. When a word takes root, it has a higher probability of living than one that is not rooted. The word must become attached to one's heart and mind so that it can obtain the substance it needs to be strengthened. This process minimizes spiritual miscarriages, abortions, and stillbirths with the word of God.

*As for* Ephraim, their glory shall fly away like a bird-- No birth, no pregnancy, and no conception! ***Hosea 9:11 (NJV)***

# 2

# Spiritual Miscarriage

Every thought that God put in the heart of man has the potential to bring forth light into dark places for the edification of others to be perfected in the body of Christ.

The loss is in the seed that never had the opportunity to give life.

When anyone hears the message about the kingdom and does not understand it, the evil one comes and snatches away what was sown in his heart. This is the seed sown along the path.
***Matthew 13:19 (NIV)***

## What is a Spiritual Miscarriage?

A Spiritual miscarriage is the loss or theft of a received word given by God before the recipient comes into full agreement with the Word of God or in the early stages of the word being development in the receiver's life.

## What Causes a Spiritual Miscarriage?

Spiritual miscarriages take place when a person has received the word of God but rejects it or cannot conceive God's word. We cannot carry anything that we do not believe in or consider gaining some understanding about it. You must believe in the word of God for it to manifest in your life. The number one cause of rejecting or not conceiving the word of God is a lack of understanding. You will always find death where there is no understanding or disbelief in the life of a believer.

> You cannot carry what you cannot conceive.

Conceiving the word of God is very vital to give spiritual birth. When the word of God cannot be conceived, it forms a blockage that hinders the word from being planted in one's heart so that it can develop roots and begin life. The word of the Lord being planted and buried within one's heart can be considered as spiritual conception. Spiritual conception is the action of conceiving a word of promise, correction, training, or purpose (child) from the Lord. Birthing out one's purpose and destiny or obtaining the promises of God is impossible without spiritual conception. The word cannot survive without being buried within the heart because it is not covered, leaving it open for the enemy to come and steal it or snatch it away from the receiver. In addition, when a word is not buried within one's heart it will not have the nutrients it needs to grow, causing a defect in its growth and development process.

Furthermore, spiritual miscarriages take place when issues arise after hearing the word of God during the delicate process of early development. Of course, this is a period where there is no full agreement within the heart and mind of the receiver of the word. The receiver can either believe in their heart, but there is doubt in their mind or vice versa. There are many occasions when an individual wants to believe the word of the Lord, and something happens that causes doubt to consume what they want to believe. This positions the receiver to be at high risk for a spiritual miscarriage. Believers must come into the understanding that one of the enemy's tactics that will lead someone to have a spiritual miscarriage is sending forth a counterfeit to attempt to discredit God's word in one's mind and heart. And when there is no full agreement with the word of the Lord, then one can easily be persuaded, and a false reality is built that it will not happen in their lives. Divisions such as these within the heart and mind of the receiver are grounds for spiritual miscarriages, as it gives room for the enemy to deceive, corrupt and infect the seed that has been released over an individual's life. This is where the enemy works very hard to accomplish contaminating the womb so that there will be no foundation for the establishment of the word. This makes it very easy for a spiritual miscarriage to go forth.

## Identifying Spiritual Miscarriages High-Risk Factors

A spiritual miscarriage is possible in the life of any believer. If the truth is told, every believer has experienced at least one in their lifetime. Many are experiencing one right now. So, if you have had one, be encouraged, you are not alone. The key here is to eliminate believers from having spiritual miscarriages. They delay and hinder promises from being obtained and purposes from being fulfilled. However, some believers have a higher probability of having a spiritual miscarriage than others due to various conditions. Here are a few risk factors that increase one's possibility of having a spiritual miscarriage.

**Spiritual Maturity:** Your maturity level in Christ can determine your likely hood of having a spiritual miscarriage. The possibility of a spiritual miscarriage is higher among those who rank low in spiritual maturity as they are more likely to reject the word of the Lord. Notice, I did not deal with spiritual age because how long you have been in Christ or how much of the bible you know does not dictate your spiritual maturity. **Your spiritual maturity level is determined by your level of willingness to carry out the word of the Lord.**

**History of Spiritual Miscarriages:** Individuals who have consistently miscarried the word of the Lord are likely to miscarry repeatedly The more you miscarry the word of the Lord the more desensitized you become at carrying it out.

**Spiritual Dysfunctions:** Individuals behavior patterns are normal to them because it's how they have always functioned. However, their behavior does not align with the word of God. We must stop making excuses for our dysfunctions as they are setting people up for spiritual miscarriages. We must function in accordance with the word of the Lord so that we can carry and birth God's glory within. **Ex.** Spiritual bipolar disorder, spiritual attention deficit hyperactivity disorder, spiritual social anxiety order, spiritual separation anxiety disorder, spiritual delusional disorder, spiritual adjustment disorder...

**Spiritual Trauma and Infections:** A fresh or old infected wound of an individual will put them at high risk for having a spiritual miscarriage. An infected wound can hinder the individual's ability to receive the word of God due to the condition or circumstance of how one acquired previous wounds. Spiritual infections cause one to have a deaf ear unto the word of the Lord, which develops a high-risk pregnancy for a spiritual miscarriage. The body is trying to heal its own wounds with self-care and all it takes is for the individual to allow the physician by the name of Jesus to tend to the wound so they can be healed from it.

**Medications:** Often people use sex, drugs, alcohol, work, etc. to medicate oneself from dealing with the emotional, mental, physical and spiritual abuse. Taking the wrong medicine can sedate or induce your level of pain and hurt from the wounds of life. Medication is a substance used for treating something. They have caused people to become addicted to substances that suppress or temporarily sedate them from the pain and hurt within. The medication's side effects can highly lead to a spiritual miscarriage as it contaminates the ability to fully conceive the word of God. Allow the word of the Lord to become our substance for treating our hurt and pain; then we can begin to conceive God's word and make spiritual conception possible in one's life.

**Toxic Environment:** Toxic environments can hinder individuals from conceiving and carrying the word of the Lord. Environmental factors that can increase your risk of miscarrying is being in the company of non-believers, places that do not cultivate your anointing, lack of faith, well stoppers, negativity, unsupportive, no room to grow (limitation), word curses, etc. If you are in a toxic environment, then you are a likely candidate for a spiritual miscarriage. A conducive environment is important for the conception and development of the Word of God.

**Paternal Traits:** Paternal traits are characteristics that we inherit from our parents. Some parents can have ungodly characteristics that one inherits, which influences a spiritual miscarriage in the life of that individual. They can come from your biological parents as well as your spiritual parents or leaders. Some paternal traits can be harmful to one's success and ability to conceive and carry out the word of the Lord only if one makes the decision to follow their parent's example(s). Paternal character traits can be unlearned and become non-effective in an individual's life. An individual must allow Jesus to be the example in which they train, learn, develop and follow as they grow into a new creation in Him.

**Spiritual Diet:** A poor spiritual diet can lead to a spiritual miscarriage due to the lack of nutrients needed for the word to survive. A poor spiritual diet consists of seeing, hearing and touching things that contaminate your temple. A mindset that is fed and influenced by the world will kill any spiritual seed. Being exposed to environments and words that are negative can highly effect your ability to comprehend and believe something positive manifesting in your life. This is an example of a poor spiritual diet. A person's diet is important to live a vibrant, healthy life, whether spiritual or physical. A change in an individual's diet can give them the substance they need to avoid a spiritual miscarriage. Individual diets can be influenced by praying, reading and studying the Word of God, being in a positive atmosphere, being in the company of positive people, etc.

## Signs of a Spiritual Miscarriage

Often, individuals cannot receive the word of God because it is contrary to their family lineage, personal history, present circumstances, and word curses they have heard before coming in contact with receiving God's word. Each of these causes the receiver to doubt and disbelieve the Word of God, giving the enemy the room he needs to come and snatch the word spoken before it can take root in the receiver's life. We should become cognizant of the different signs of a spiritual miscarriage so that an individual can be prevented from having one.

**Spiritual Ignorance:** Spiritual ignorance is the lack of knowledge and understanding of spiritual matters. If an individual is given a word and they cannot understand it instantly, this conditions the word to be miscarried. Isaiah 5:13 talks about God's people dying from hunger and thirst because of their lack of understanding.

Death is the result of a word wherever there is a lack of understanding.

Understanding a word gives the individual the information they need to decide to accept or reject it. A word that is not understood cannot be carried or given birth to due to the limitation of the individual's ability to decide beyond themselves. Understanding brings forth the beginning of life. To overcome spiritual ignorance, the individual's mindset must be renewed in the Word of God. **Romans: 12:2**

Knowledge informs you, understanding reforms you and wisdom conforms you.

**Infections:** lack of understanding and knowledge, selfishness, rebellion, lack of discipline, the hardness of heart, spiritual blindness, spiritually deaf, lack of discernment, spiritually dead, pride, etc.

**Ways to overcome spiritual ignorance.**
- ❖ Have a receptive heart and mind focused on God. *Proverbs 2:2-5*
- ❖ Build an intimate relationship with God. *Ephesians 1:17*
- ❖ Seek God for understanding. *Jeremiah 33:3*
- ❖ Search the word of God. *Psalm 119:130*
- ❖ Obtain wise, godly counsel. *Proverbs 15:22*
- ❖ Grow in the grace of God. *2 Peter 3:18*
- ❖ Meditate on it. *2 Timothy 2:7; Joshua 1:8*
- ❖ Study to show yourself approved. *2 Timothy 2:15*

## Prenatal Visit

**Scripture Study:** Read Exodus 4 & 5     **Person:** Pharaoh

**Assignment**

What events led to Pharaoh being a high-risk factor for a spiritual miscarriage?

_____   _____   _____
_____   _____   _____

What infections can determine Pharaoh's diagnosis that led him to having a spiritual miscarriage?

_____   _____   _____
_____   _____   _____

Reflect on the Egyptian's outcome from the 10 plagues due to Pharaoh's reaction and responses to Moses during every visit. Can you identify somethings that Pharaoh could have done different to change the outcome for the Egyptians?

_____
_____
_____
_____
_____

Are there areas in your life where you can identify experiencing spiritual ignorance? If so, how can you overcome them?

_____
_____

**Spiritually bleeding** – Spiritual bleeding is the hemorrhaging of the heart from the pain and hurt that one has accumulated throughout life, which has not been healed. This is where the enemy targets his flaming arrows. Many are wounded, suffering in silence and hiding behind masks that conceal the hurt and pain within due to unsuccessful relationships, negative words, family upbringing, broken promises, church hurt, physical, sexual, and emotional abuse that blemishes their confidence in just words. This invisible outpouring is where doubt, distrust, or lack of faith settles in from the issues of life that causes one to have a spiritual miscarriage because they don't have the strength to hold it. One cannot take another disappointment, let down, abuse, neglect, or manipulation so, they choose to dismiss even the truth. It is like pouring new wine into old wineskin that will burst because it does not have the capacity to hold the new wine. Unfortunately, we treat God and His word as if it was given by mankind. Man is fallible; God is infallible. Therefore, we cannot handle or charge God according to the mistakes made by man. Instead, we must embrace God and build a relationship with Him by allowing Him into every place of our lives. And yes, even the secret places that we cover up and mask the pain and hurt within our hearts.

He heals the brokenhearted and binds up their wounds.

*Psalm 147:3 (NIV)*

**Infections:** Doubt, Disbelief, distrust, discouragement, fear, jealousy, envy, covetousness, torment, hopeless, mockery, unforgiveness, grudges, stressed, rejection, failure, pride, harden hearts, grief, insecurities, etc.

Spiritual Miscarriage

**Ways to overcome spiritual bleeding.**

- ❖ Cry out to God about your pain. *Psalm 6:2*
- ❖ Trust God with your hurt and pain. *Psalm 51:17*
- ❖ Meditate on God's word. *Psalms 3:2*
- ❖ Forget the former things. *Isaiah 43:18-19*
- ❖ He heals hearts and wounds. *Psalm 147*
- ❖ He will revive you. *Isaiah 57:15*
- ❖ Forgive those who have hurt you. *Matthew 6:14*
- ❖ Try God at His word. *James 1:22*
- ❖ Cast your cares unto the Lord. *1 Peter 5:7*

Abortions "In The Church" Divine Strategies to Spiritual Deliverance

## *Prenatal Visit*

**Scripture Study:** Read 1 Samuel 1          **Person**: Hannah

**Assignment**

What high-risk factors can you diagnose Hannah with that made her minimize and miscarry Elkanah's love for her?

- ❏ Spiritual Maturity
- ❏ History of Spiritual Miscarriages
- ❏ Spiritual Dysfunctions
- ❏ Spiritual Trauma and Infections
- ❏ Medications
- ❏ Paternal Traits
- ❏ Toxic Environment
- ❏ Spiritual Diet
- ❏ _____

Can you diagnose the infections in Hannah's life that caused her to reject the love of Elkanah?

_____   _____   _____

_____   _____   _____

_____   _____   _____

What influences do you believed influenced Hannah's behavior and desire to give birth to a son?

_____
_____
_____

How did Hannah overcome her situation?

_____
_____
_____
_____
_____

**Spiritual Torment** – Spiritual torment is when an individual is tortured by the enemy within the mind through the overpowering of suggestive thoughts of temptation, accusations, or deception that leads to becoming the word. This is where the toothless lion, known as the devil or the author of confusion, roars or speaks all types of words of negativity. Some examples of spiritual torment are lies, accusations, questioning your abilities, reminding you about past mistakes, family history, failures, or disappointments, so that one can be blinded from seeing or believing they can accomplish the word of the Lord. He tries to lure you into old activities and patterns of behaviors through suggestions or images. The toothless lion plays on your history to paralyze your presence in the effort to stop your future.

The weapons we fight with are not the weapons of the world. On the contrary, they have divine power to demolish strongholds. We demolish arguments and every pretension that sets itself up against the knowledge of God, and we take captive every thought to make it obedient to Christ. And we will be ready to punish every act of disobedience, once your obedience is complete.
**2 Corinthians 10:4-6 (NIV)**

When we hold on to or entertain such things, we become paralyzed and have a spiritual miscarriage. That's why we are called to cast down imaginations and every high thing that exalts itself against the knowledge of God and brings into captivity every thought and makes it obedient to Christ Jesus. Failing to do this will cause one to be in places of condemnation, intimidation, insecurities, division, etc.

**Infections:** condemnation, intimidation, insecurities, division, self-hate, low self-esteem, guilt, shame, depression, oppression, suicidal thoughts, worthlessness, doubt, fear, unforgiveness, grudges, rejection, failure, pride, jealousy, procrastination, etc.

**Ways to overcome spiritual torment.**
- Be renewed in the spirit of your mind. *Ephesians 4:23*
- Set your mind on the things above. *Colossians 3:2*
- Think on things that are true and pure. *Philippians 4:8*
- Purify your soul. *1 Peter 1.22*
- Know that God is faithful. *Deuteronomy 7:9*
- Learn the word of God. *Psalm 119:15-16*
- Reject fear. *2 Timothy 1:7*
- Know that you have been given the victory. *Psalm 44:7*
- Decree God's word. *Job 22:28*
- Rebuke the enemy. *James 4:7*
- Stand firm on God's word. *Exodus 14:13*
- Be confident. *Psalm 27:3*
- Put trust in God. *Psalm 62:8*
- Have assurance in God. *Psalms 13:4; Romans 8:38-29;*

## Prenatal Visit

**Scripture Study:** Read Esther 3  **Person:** Haman

**Assignment**

What high-risk factors can you diagnose Haman with that made him miscarry his purpose and position in the kingdom?

- ❏ Spiritual Maturity
- ❏ History of Spiritual Miscarriages
- ❏ Spiritual Dysfunctions
- ❏ Spiritual Trauma and Infections
- ❏ _____

- ❏ Medications
- ❏ Paternal Traits
- ❏ Toxic Environment
- ❏ Spiritual Diet

What events led to Haman early termination of his purpose and position in the kingdom?

_____
_____
_____
_____

Diagnose any infections that contributed to Haman having a spiritual miscarriage with his purpose.

_____   _____   _____

_____   _____   _____

_____   _____   _____

Provide some medical reference notes that can prevent Haman's outcome from happening to another patient.

_____
_____
_____
_____
_____

## Spiritual Miscarriage Prevention Methods

This is a very critical moment in the life of the receiver as it can cause one to move forth in destiny or miscarry their destiny. It's important that the giver of the word of God or designees pray for the individual's ability to receive the word of God and break any demonic influences that would hinder one from receiving it. It's also important for the (spiritual midwife) leader or disciple of the receiver of the word (especially for babes in Christ) to hear or obtain a copy of that word so that they too can keep that person covered in prayer and be available to pray, counsel, and guide them to prevent a spiritual miscarriage. The receiver of the word should not dismiss the word given, despite all that has happened or been said to them up to that point.

But test them all, hold on to what is good, reject every kind of evil.
**1 Thessalonians 5:21-22(NIV)**

The receiver should

- Not dismiss the word of God
- Write down the word that has been given to them
- Pray over the word that has been given
- Ask God for clarity of the word
- Seek godly counsel of the word from your spiritual midwife (leader).
- Watch for the word to manifest itself
- Judge the word
  - How to judge is the word is from the Lord
    - It will not violate the word of God
    - It will not lead you to sin against God

**Agreement:** A very critical component of preventing a spiritual miscarriage is in the power of agreement. An agreement is an act of agreeing or of coming to a mutual agreement by all parties. A word cannot be carried, nurtured and birth full term unless there is a mutual agreement. When there is no full agreement with the word, it makes it easy for the enemy to come and snatch the word from the receiver. Two cannot walk together unless there is an agreement because one will be doing one thing and the other will be doing something else, and nothing will be accomplished. God sends forth his word to accomplish and establish things in the lives of His children.

> ➢ The first level of agreement must be within your heart and mind. The two of these must touch and agree with one another so that the word can survive the term of the spiritual pregnancy. A division within the heart and mind opens the door for the enemy to deceive, corrupt and infect the seed for a spiritual miscarriage to go forth of the word that has been released over the receiver's life. If the two of these do not agree, you will always be considered high risk of having a spiritual miscarriage. The receiver is considered high risk because the one that is not in agreement with the word of the Lord will always bring forth conflict or cause confusion concerning the word. It will always try to talk the other into believing its views. You will find the disagreeable component operating under spiritual ignorance, bleeding or torment because of its condition(s).

> ➢ When your heart and mind touch and agree on the things of God, there is nothing that can stop the word from coming to pass. God requires two things to agree before it can manifest. The Holy Spirit will come upon you and overshadow you when you have an agreement of the

heart and the mind. With the Holy Spirit upon you, there has been a three-stranded cord agreement between your mind, heart, and spirit of the Lord. The Holy Spirit is always in agreement with the Lord. The Spirit of the Lord is always waiting for us to come into the agreement with God's word. It is only when there's a breach of the agreement that will hinder a word from coming to pass.

The mind is a recorder of thoughts and words and the heart is a recorder of wounds and injuries

the sinful mind is hostile to God. It does not submit to God's law, nor can it do so.. **Romans 8:7 (NIV)**

➢ How to get the heart and mind on one accord. Buy the truth and do not sell it gaining wisdom, knowledge, and understanding according to **Proverbs 23:23.**
- o Pray to God for understanding and for God to help your unbelief.
- o Search the scriptures dealing with the areas that you are struggling or hindering your belief.
- o Study and meditate on those scriptures.
- o Speak out loud the word of the Lord as faith comes by hearing.
- o Pray for deliverance from any root problems that are causing the disbelief and hindrances.
- o Seek Godly counsel.
- o Disassociate yourself with people, things, and environments that are not conducive for the

growth and development of God's word in your life.
- A divided house cannot stand.

Note; The word of the Lord is like the hammer and it will break up all fallow ground so that it can become fertile. Let God break up the fallow ground.

**Additional Scriptures for meditations**

- ❖ Accept the truth. *1 Thessalonians 2:13*
- ❖ Receive God's word of healing. *Psalm 107:20*
- ❖ Ask God to help your unbelief. *Mark 9:24*
- ❖ Believe *John 20:27, John 14:1*
- ❖ Be content. *1 Timothy 6:6*
- ❖ Allow God to sustain you. *Psalm 3:1-8*
- ❖ Allow the Word to cleanse you. *John 15:3*
- ❖ Allow God's word to deliver you. *Psalm 107.20*
- ❖ Speak the word of God over your life. *Romans 10:17*
- ❖ Take Courage. *Psalm 27:13-14*
- ❖ Study the word of God.
- ❖ Don't be afraid. *Isaiah 41:10*
- ❖ Stop looking for man's validation. *Galatians 1:10*
- ❖ Trust Gods work within you. *Psalm 139:13-14*
- ❖ Don't get distracted. *Psalm 119:15*
- ❖ Find, eat and become God's word. *Jeremiah 15:16*
- ❖ Humble yourself. *1 Peter 5:6*
- ❖ Trust God with your heart. *Proverbs 3:5*
- ❖ Cast your cares unto the Lord. *1 Peter 5:7*
- ❖ God will bind up your wounds. *Ezekiel 34:16*

When the mind and heart unify on one accord it has the capacity to be fruitful, multiply and subdue the earth.

## Exercise:

**Read:** Proverbs 3:5 "Trust in the lord with all thy heart and lean not to thine own understanding, acknowledge him in all thy ways and he shall direct your path"

In the scripture Proverbs 3:5 what did the psalmist say we must do concerning the Lord?

_____

And how must we do it?

_____

Why do you believe the psalmist made the statement concerning our own understanding?

_____
_____
_____
_____
_____
_____
_____

List three things that the Lord has spoken to you about what you are questioning or do not believe.

1. _____
2. _____
3. _____

Honestly, write down the reason you are questioning or do not believe what God has spoken.

1. _____
_____
_____
_____

2. _____
   _____
   _____
   _____

3. _____
   _____
   _____
   _____

Does your reasoning make you a high-risk candidate for a spiritual miscarriage? ❑ Yes ❑No

What is your risk factor? ❑ Spiritual Maturity ❑History of Spiritual Miscarriages ❑ Spiritual Dysfunctions ❑ Spiritual Trauma and Infections ❑ Medications ❑ Toxic Environment ❑ Paternal Traits ❑ Spiritual Diet ❑_____

Which category do you fall under in the signs of a spiritual miscarriage?

❑ Spiritual Ignorance ❑Spiritual Bleeding ❑Spiritual Torment

List areas of infections for the signs of a spiritual miscarriage.

_____   _____   _____

_____   _____   _____

_____   _____   _____

How can you overcome these signs?

1. _____
   _____
   _____

2. _____

3. _____

What methods can you use to prevent from having a spiritual miscarriage?

1. _____
2. _____
3. _____
4. _____
5. _____

Find and write down three scriptures that deal with one of your areas of infections: Ex. Insecurities -Psalms 139:14.

1. _____
2. _____
3. _____

Spiritual Miscarriage

Pray unto the Lord concerning the areas of infection and where you first encountered it.

Forgive anyone that may have hurt you.

Meditate on scripture that deals with the area of infection. Psalms 1:3

Write down how these scriptures speak to you personally.

1. _____
   _____
   _____
   _____

2. _____
   _____
   _____
   _____

3. _____
   _____
   _____
   _____

Repeat this exercise for each of those infectious areas.

---

As the heavens are higher than the earth, so are my ways higher than your ways and my thoughts than your thoughts. **Isaiah 55:9 (NIV)**

**Prayer**

Heavenly Father, I come to you, with a humble spirit, a heart full of thanksgiving and mouth full of praise because you are a phenomenal God. A God who is everywhere (omnipresent), all knowing (om·nis·cient), and all powerful omnipotent.

Lord, boldly I stand asking for forgiveness of my sins known and unknown, including my doubt, lack of trust, unfaithfulness to you. I rise today as your seed of righteousness to be planted firmly in you like the tree planted by streams of water, which yields its fruit in season, whose leaf does not wither. And prosper in every way as it is written in Psalms 1:3. So I can accept the fullness of your seed, precious Lord, I call every fallow ground to be broken up because your seeds shall not be sown among thorns. I recognize that even the fallow grounds within me must be plowed so that your precious seeds will not be miscarried. Every unplowed ground must be plowed so that your graciously seeds will be accepted (conceived). As the fallow grounds in my life are broken up let righteousness be sown within me, let me reap in mercy. I am seeking you Father until you come and rain righteousness in my life. Wickedness has been plowed within my life, I have reaped iniquities, I have eaten the fruit of lies because I didn't trust in you. Lord, help my unbelief in the name of Jesus.

Today is a new day, a new year and it is in you that I trust, I decree that all lies are demolished for I am buying back your truth and we will never sell it again. I cover my purpose, visions, dreams, etc. with the blood of Jesus. I decree that I am cleansed from iniquities because of your rain of righteousness, full of grace and mercy is upon me. I uproot every seed of wickedness, doubt, lack of trust, unfaithfulness, deception, etc. within me as the fallow ground is being broken up. I destroy every emotion tie within the memory of our heart, mind, and loins that have caused us to reject your word to return no more in Jesus name. It is your word that brings forth life dear God and I choose life and life abundantly as your Son and my Savior Jesus Christ has given unto me. I lift your name up God, as I walk om your truth that has set me free. that we shall walk in freedom in as the truth sets us free.

I worship you, Lord, that the fallow ground is broken up in my heart is fertile ground for your seed of righteousness to be sown. I thank you, Father, in the name of Jesus, the t fertile ground has come forth, my ears and eyes have been opened to receive your word. I magnify you, that I will no longer be put to shame; neither will my face grow pale as I acknowledge you. I praise you that for gaining understanding and accepting your instruction without complaints.

I praise you Lord for your word that cleanses us. I glorify your name for the rain that cleanses us in the name of Jesus. I magnify you, Lord, that your word is like a hammer that breaks a rock into pieces. I thank you, Lord, that your word is living and active. Sharper than any double-edged sword, it penetrates even to dividing soul and spirit, joints and marrow; it judges the thoughts and attitudes of the heart. I worship you, Father, as your Spirit is poured upon me from on high, and the deserted fields become fertile and the fertile fields seem like a forest that justices will dwell in the desert and righteousness will live in the fertile fields. I praise your name that the fruit of righteousness will be peace and the effect of righteousness will be quietness and confidence forever, I thank you, Lord, that I will live in peaceful dwelling places, in secure homes, and I will have undisturbed places of rest in Jesus name.

I will give you a new heart and put a new spirit in you; I will remove from you your heart of stone and give you a heart of flesh. And I will put my Spirit in you and move you to follow my decrees and be careful to keep my laws.

**Ezekiel 36:26-27 (NIV)**

I bless your name Lord that I can draw near to you with a sincere heart in full assurance of faith, having our hearts sprinkled to cleanse us from a guilty conscience and having our bodies washed with pure water. In the name of Jesus, I pray. Amen, Amen, & Amen

## ❧ Notes & Prayer Requests ☙

# 3

# Spiritual Abortion

Fear of God will cause you to **FULFILL** your destiny
and the fear of man will cause you to **ABORT** your destiny

The one who received the seed that fell on rocky places is the man who hears the word and at once receives it with joy. But since he has no root, he lasts only a short time. When trouble or persecution comes because of the word, he quickly falls away.
***Matthew 13:20-21 (NIV)***

## What is a Spiritual Abortion?

A spiritual abortion is defined as the termination of a God-given assignment, whether induced or spontaneous by the recipient of God's word that results in them not completing or carrying out their assignment from God.

## What causes Spiritual Abortions?

Spiritual Abortions take place when an individual receives a word from God that they believe to the extent of moving on God's spoken word unto them. They find themselves actively engaged in God's word in their life for a period and abruptly or gradually terminate the assignment before its completion due to one or more circumstances.

Do not conform any longer to the pattern of this world, but be transformed by the renewing of your mind. Then you will be able to test and approve what God's will is--his good, pleasing and perfect will. **Romans 12:2 (NIV)**

When a word is released to a receiver, this is called the conception period. The individual is delighted and excited to be on assignment from the Lord. The receiver at this stage comes into an agreement with God's word about their life within their heart, mind or both. Because the individual has come into unity with the word of God in some form, now the process of carrying out the word can begin. At that point, the receiver's intentions are to follow through with God's assignment for their life. When something happens to change the individual's mind and/or heart on following through with their assignment from God, a spiritual abortion takes place. The abortion could have been induced or happened spontaneously due to the receiver's personal thoughts, past or present situation, peers, society or environmental influences.

Spiritual abortions that are induced take place when an individual is influenced, persuaded, encouraged, provoked, or suggested continually to abort one's assignment and the individual agrees or conforms to it. Negative environments and people's lack of support, mockery, ridicule, or rejection are some influencing factors that can cause and induced abortion. These are intentional acts used for the purpose of causing the receiver to abort God's word. Induced abortions are triggered in a progressive manner, usually from reoccurring events into the receivers' life until its intended purpose is complete. Reoccurring events influence the recipient of God's word to decrease engagement in the word until the receive completely disengages from their assignment. Understand that the enemy never aborts his assignments. That's why it is our responsibility to stand firm on the word of God until His word comes to pass in our life.

Spontaneously spiritual abortions take place when a sudden decision is made to terminate their assignment due to unexpected circumstances that seem beyond the carrier's capacity to carry out the word. It occurs during an event, situation or circumstance or immediately afterward. Spontaneous abortions are not delayed or prolonged because they are stimulated by impulsive behaviors. This happens when the counterfeit situation is illuminated in the eyes of the carrier in such a way that they believe that it is impossible for them to complete the task.

A condition that causes a receiver to be subject to a spiritual abortion is called a faulty foundation or simply no roots. A faulty foundation arises when your relationship with God is based on your desires and not His will and your love for Him. In this condition, you know about God, but you have not come to a definite relationship with God in either all or parts of your life. It's a place where you are not rooted or grounded in God and His word. This is also where individuals operate in a form a godliness but deny the power of God to work and manifest in one's life. This state has not only caused individuals to abort their assignments but also have caused many to abort their faith and God.

One key component that is missing in an individual's life who is susceptible to having a spiritual abortion is a personal relationship with God. The greater the relationship, the less susceptible one becomes to living on a faulty foundation. A personal relationship with God gives us the confidence we need to be rooted, planted and assured in God and His word. It builds our faith and positions us to have a faith in action, a faith that acts on God's word alone.

Very frequently, when an abortion takes place, the individual who is expecting or carrying the seed does not want to abort the word. But due to the condition of their environment or company kept and other high-risk factors, they abort the assignment.

## Identifying Spiritual Abortions High-Risk Factors

There are several underlying reasons and high-risk factors that cause individuals to have spiritual abortions. Throughout history and even now believers are having them at alarming rates. It is a part of the dysfunctions that are taking place within the body of Christ. Our role here is to eliminate believers from contemplating and having spiritual abortions. As we release spiritual knowledge to equip believers in identifying high-risk factors that influence individuals in having a spiritual abortion.

Some conditions increase the probability of an individual having a spiritual abortion more than others. We will identify a few risk factors that contribute to individual's aborting their God-given assignment and leading them to unclaimed promises and unfulfilled lives to reduce and eliminate spiritual abortions in the lives of believers. Some common high-risk factors are:

**History**: A pattern of having a spiritual abortion can cause an individual to become comfortable with them and increase the likelihood of them carrying out another one. People whose history increases their risk toward a spiritual abortion should find an accountability partner to decrease this factor. Have you found yourself in a state of starting things but never completing them?

If your answer is yes, then you have just been identified as having a history of spiritual abortions. Due to this fact, you need to have an accountability partner (spiritual midwife) who will coach you through to completion (delivery).

**Toxic Environment:** A toxic environment can produce an induced abortion in the life of an individual. It can increase the risk of the individual's ability to carry out the word of God because it is set up to consistently plant words or events that focus on limitations and hindrances. Those who are in it can be persuaded, provoked, or influenced to terminate their pregnancy by several environmental factors. Some factors include: no spiritual support of God's word for your life, the word over your life is being challenged, cursed or spoken negatively about, and faith limitations. Toxic environments cause individuals to lose focus on what is possible with God as it gives vital attention to their own strength and others abilities. Individuals must remove themselves from toxic environments to decrease the possibility of a spiritual abortion taking place within their lives.

**Spiritual Trauma and Infections:** Traumatic episodes or incidents that are associated with any form of fear, admonition, mortification, repudiation, approval, etc. can cause individuals to be a high-risk candidates for a spiritual abortion. These types of behaviors can cause a fresh wound or trigger the opening of an old wound that causes individuals to terminate their assignment. The depth of the wound will determine if the individual will have a spontaneous or induced abortion.

Spontaneous abortion is usually caused by incidents that develop deep wounds and/or reopen old wounds that have not been healed. Abortions that are induced by traumatic episodes are usually caused by situations that consistently dig in already existing wound causing repeated and deeper pain. Individuals who receive traumatic episodes of this effect should deal with the healing process of their wounds, stop taking things so personally, stand on God's word alone, and don't submit to being a victim of this type of abuse. They should not build or put the dependence of the delivery of their assignment (visions, goals, dreams, etc.) around the acceptance and/or support of others. In addition, they should surround themselves with those who are supportive to the what they are carrying so the individual will not abort their baby or cause their baby to have any birth defects.

**Man pleasing/People Bondage**: Having the desire to please man can increase the chances of an individual having a spiritual abortion. This is a risk factor because it can cause an individual to abort the word of God or instructions if the person they desire to please does not agree with God's word. Being in the bondage of people will set up an individual to abort a personal word from God and especially an assignment that concerns the individual whom they desire to please. We must be freed from people if we expect to carry out God's word for our personal lives and assignments as it pertains to others. God's word must become more important to us than the words of others.

**Self-Sabotage:** Behavior or habits that individuals display that hinder, restrict or create problems in completing an assignment are called self-sabotage. People operating under these patterns of behaviors are at high risk for having a spiritual abortion because they will consciously or subconsciously cause problems that influence an induced abortion. These people are very crafty in finding ways to stop themselves from completing their assignment.

A few forms of self-sabotage behaviors/patterns are procrastinating, self-medicating, self-injury, comfort eating, helplessness, lack of self-dependency, self-derogation, etc. These behavior patterns promote a cycle of spiritual abortion. Individuals who have any of these behavior patterns can overcome and conquer them through their relationship with God and His word. Building a relationship with God will help the individual overcome identity issues, and come into who they are and their capacity in Christ Jesus

**Toxic Emotions/Hormonal change/ Unstable emotions:** Emotions cause individuals to be very unstable if they do not obtain control over them. Individuals who are controlled by their emotions are at a very high risk of having a spiritual abortion. When a person's emotions determine their actions, this can be very dangerous to carry the word out to completion. It is dangerous because the individual's response to the word at any given time is conditional and could lead to aborting the word spontaneously. The carrier of the word cannot allow conditions to dictate their decision to carry out the word. One must make a commitment to stand on the word no matter what takes place and follow through with it until the end, so the word can take root, nurture, and grow.

"Watch and pray so that you will not fall into temptation. The spirit is willing, but the body is weak."
*Matthew 26:41 (NIV)*

## Warning Signs of Spiritual Abortions

When an individual receives and conceives a word from God, they often find themselves in the valley of decision, whether to keep moving in the delivery of God's word or to abort it. The reasons for being in this valley of decision could be numerous and possible threats to one's mind. Therefore, hindering their ability to deliver God's word. Then there are other times where circumstances cause an individual to spontaneously abort the word that God has given them without even having the option to decide rationally. Whether one is on the verge of a spontaneous or induced abortion, some signs could assist an individual from having the act to take place within their assignment from God. It is important that we become more aware of the different warning signs of a spiritual abortion so that one can take proactive preventive measures. We will discuss a few warning signs within this section.

**Spiritual Disengaged:** Spiritual disengagement is the action or process of withdrawing or separating from involvement in an assignment from God. This separation can take place physically and emotionally. Individuals will disengage themselves from their assignment when they are consistently denied cultivation of God's word, ignored and overlooked, or not supported, and it will result in a spiritual abortion. According to the book of Jeremiah, there was a time in his walk when he wanted to abort his assignment due to the backlash, abuse, imprisonment, being ignored, insults, or threats. Jeremiah got to the point where he said he was not even going to mention God's name anymore. However, because Jeremiah had the word of God in his heart it was like fire, and he could not hold back. ***Jeremiah 20:9***

**Infections:** rejection, slothfulness, laziness, procrastination, fear, invaluable, low self-esteem, insecurities, lack of confidence, worthlessness, discouragement, depression, death, shut down, broken spirit, etc.

**Ways to overcome spiritual disengagement.**

- Press toward the mark. ***Philippians 3:14***
- Be diligent. ***Proverbs 10:4, 12:24, 13:4, 21:5, Galatians 6:9***
- Set your mind on Christ. ***Hebrews 3:1***
- Be confident in God. ***Philippians 1:6***
- Christ will sustain you. ***1 Corinthians 1:8***
- Your work is not in vain. ***Philippians 2:16***
- Be strengthened by God's word. ***Psalm 119:28***
- Accompany yourself with encouragers. ***1 Thessalonians 5:11, Romans 1:12***
- Be steadfast. ***1 Corinthians 15:58***

**Abortions "In The Church" Divine Strategies to Spiritual Deliverance**

## *Prenatal Visit*

**Scripture Study:** Read *Jeremiah 20*  **Person**: Jeremiah

**Assignment**

Can you identify factors that contribute to the Prophet Jeremiah being a potential spiritual abortion candidate?

_____  _____  _____

What events led to Jeremiah being a high-risk factor for a spiritual abortion?

_____
_____
_____
_____

What area of infections can you detect which indicate that Jeremiah can potentially have a spiritual abortion?

_____  _____  _____
_____  _____  _____

Did Jeremiah overcome the danger of spiritual abortion
❏ Yes ❏ No

What contributed to Jeremiah's outcome?

_____
_____
_____
_____
_____

**Spiritual Bigamy/Adultery**: Individuals who are trying to be in covenant with God and the world are at high risk of having a spiritual abortion because one cannot serve two masters. Just like one cannot have two husbands or wives because it will always bring conflict between the two. The things of God are spiritual, and the things of the world are flesh. The two are always at war with one another. For this reason, one will abort the word of God if their fleshly desire is stronger than their spiritual desire. That which pleases their flesh will always talk them into having a spiritual abortion.

God became angry with King Solomon because his heart turned from God and unto the gods of his wives. Israel was commanded not to intermarry with other nations as they would turn their hearts unto their gods. King Solomon did not keep the commandment of God as he had seven hundred wives, princesses, and three hundred concubines from several different nations. These women influenced King Solomon and turned his heart toward their gods, and he was no longer loyal to God. According to 1 King 11:11-12, this physical act of bigamy and adultery was a reflection of his spiritual actions, and it caused the kingdom to be torn away from his sons and given to his servant.

**Infections:** covetousness, pride, greed, lust, fornication, adultery, envy, jealousy, self-indulgence, debauchery, double-minded, lack of trust, doubtful, insecurities, deceitful, uncertainty, lack of confidence, rejection,

**Ways to overcome spiritual bigamy.**

- Choose who you are going to serve. *Joshua 24:14 -15*
- Purify your sight. *Matthew 6:22-23*
- Despise/Hate Sin. *Psalm 97:10*
- Don't be a lover of money. *1 Timothy 6:9-12*
- Don't fear man. *Hebrews 13:5-6*
- Store up treasures in heaven. *Matthew 6:19-21*
- Do not love the things of this world. *1 John 2:15-1*
- Put to death your earthly nature. *Colossians 3:4-7*
- Keep God's word. *John 14:23-24*

**Abortions "In The Church" Divine Strategies to Spiritual Deliverance**

## *Prenatal Visit*

**Scripture Study:** Read *1 King 11*      **Person**: King Solomon

**Assignment**

What events lead to King Solomon being a high-risk patient for a spiritual abortion?

_____
_____
_____
_____

How did spiritual bigamy / adultery play a major role in King Solomon's outcome?

_____
_____
_____
_____

What area of infections if any can you diagnose that contributed to King Solomon's outcome?

_____    _____    _____
_____    _____    _____

Provide some medical reference notes that can prevent King Solomon's outcome from happening to another patient.

_____
_____
_____
_____
_____

**Spiritual Codependency** – Spiritual Codependency is a dysfunctional relationship where one person's unhealthy behaviors support or enables another person's unhealthy manners. The enabler believes that they are helping the one that they are supporting but in reality, they are hindering them from growing in or birthing God's purpose for them. Spiritual codependency is a setup for spiritual abortions because it doesn't promote accountability or responsibility to oneself or purpose.

The priest Eli and his sons had a very dysfunctional relationship that was damaging the office of the priesthood as they misrepresented God. Eli's sons were corrupted because they did not know the Lord as they failed to commit their lives to following Him. There was an absence of a personal relationship between Eli's sons and God. This caused them to omit the priest's customs for proper sacrifices and other wicked behavior before God. They took God's portion of the sacrifice and threatened the people who objected their wrong behavior. Finally, Eli slightly rebuked his sons and failed to cease their sinful behavior. Their father's earlier silence led to the increase of their wickedness before God as it appeared, as a supportive response. Therefore, it hindered his attempt to rebuke and stop their behavior. God sent an unnamed prophet to pronounce the word and judgment of God, and then reiterated it through the prophet Samuel. However, because of the codependency relationship between Eli and his sons, he did not listen to the announcement or judgment of God, and it led to the death of the male seeds of his family.

**Infections:** slothfulness, idleness, helpless, abandoned, defenseless, unworthiness, victim, addiction, manipulation, deception, indulgence, blame, impostor, unreliable, inconsistent, negligence, inattention, idolatry

**Ways to overcome spiritual codependency**

- ➢ Depend only on Christ. *Psalm 16:8 John 15:5*
- ➢ Trust the Lord. *Jeremiah 17:7*
- ➢ Be crucified with Christ. *Galatians 2:20*
- ➢ Rely on God. *2 Corinthians 1:8-9*

- ➢ Become rooted in Christ. **Colossians 2:7**
- ➢ Call upon the Lord. **Psalm 18:6**
- ➢ Become a living sacrifice. **Roman 12:1**
- ➢ Renew your mind. **Roman 12:2**
- ➢ Turn from the proud. **Psalm 40:3-4**
- ➢ Demolish idols. **2 King 23**
- ➢ Take responsibility for your actions. **2 Samuel 12:13**
- ➢ Be accountable. **Romans 14:12, Jeremiah 17:10**
- ➢ Trust in God. **Psalm 37:4-6**
- ➢ Obey the Lord. **John 14:15, Luke 11:28**
- ➢ Seek God. **1 Chronicles 16:11, Jeremiah 29:11-14**
- ➢ Be diligent in God's work. **Proverbs 21:5, 2 Chronicles 24:13**
- ➢ Be open to correction. **Proverbs 27:5-6**
- ➢ Give thoughts to your words. **Matthew 12:36-37**
- ➢ Find accountability partners. **Proverbs 27:17**
- ➢ Set your mind on the things above. **Colossians 3:1-2**
- ➢ Hold one another accountable. **James 5:16**
- ➢ Build you faith. **Romans 10:17**
- ➢ Lead others to Jesus. **Acts 4:12**
- ➢ Train children (natural and spiritual) in the ways of the Lord. **Proverbs 22:6**

The man with the two talents also came. 'Master,' he said, 'you entrusted me with two talents; see, I have gained two more.' "His master replied, 'Well done, good and faithful servant! You have been faithful with a few things; I will put you in charge of many things. Come and share your master's happiness!'

**Matthew 25:22-23 (NIV)**

## *Prenatal Visit*

**Scripture Study:** Read 1 Samuel 2 & 1 Samuel 4

**Person:** Eli & his two sons, Hophni and Phinehas

**Assignment**

Upon examining Eli and his sons who would you consider responsible for them having a spiritual abortion?
_____

Diagnosed high-risk factors that contributed to this spiritual abortion.
_____   _____   _____
_____   _____   _____

What area of infections can you identify that leads to the diagnoses of a spiritual abortion?
_____   _____   _____
_____   _____   _____

What can you take away from this experience that would assist you in not contributing to spiritual codependency?
_____
_____
_____
_____

## Spiritual Abortion Prevention Methods

The fear of God is the beginning of wisdom and to depart from evil is understanding. Job 28:28

The fear of God is not only the beginning of wisdom; it is the number one spiritual abortion preventive method. As it combats the number one cause of spiritual abortions, which is various forms of fear. Operating in any kind of fear outside of the fear of God hinders your ability to submit and serve God. Fear hinders faith from operating in your life and will cause you to abort the word of God. According to 1 Samuel 15:24, Saul aborted his assignment from God because he feared man. This very act caused God to reject Saul and reduced kingship for his children to one tribe within God's kingdom.

For God, did not give us a spirit of timidity, but a spirit of power, of love and of self-discipline.
**2 Timothy 1:7 (NIV)**

On the contrary, the fear of God will prompt us to move in faith and obedience and birth out God's word. To prevent from having a spiritual abortion, the carrier of God's word must fear God more than they fear anything else. Wisdom speaks very loudly as it is the mother of all learning and it teaches us how to overcome various forms of fear.

- ❖ **Overcome the fear of failure.**
  - You will be successful. ***Joshua 1:8***
  - You can do all things through Christ. **Philippian 4:13**
- ❖ **Overcome the fear of the unknown.**
  - Dwell in the shadow of the Almighty. ***Psalms 91***
  - Be obedient. ***Hebrews 11:8***
- ❖ **Overcome the fear of people.**

- o Stop regarding man. *Isaiah 2:22*
- o Please God. *1 Thessalonians 2:4*
- ❖ **Overcome the fear of pain.**
  - o Fix your eyes on what is unseen. *2 Corinthians 4:16-18*
  - o Don't deny God's word. *Job 6:10*
- ❖ **Overcome the fear of death.**
  - o No one can stand against you. *Romans 8:31*
  - o Make God your stronghold. *Psalm 27:1*
  - o Be faithful and obtain your victor's crown. *Revelation 2:10*
  - o Fear no evil. *Psalm 23:4*
- ❖ **Overcome the fear of rejection.**
  - o Trust in the Lord. *Proverbs 29:25*
  - o You are approved by God. *2 Corinthians 10:18*
  - o You don't need man's recommendation. *2 Corinthians 3:1*
- ❖ **Overcome the fear of ridicule.**
  - o God cannot be mocked. *Galatians 6:7*
  - o Consider it pure joy. *James 1:2-4*
- ❖ **Overcome the fear of disappointment.**
  - o Guard your heart and mind. *Philippians 4:6-7*
  - o Hope in God. *Psalm 43:5*

Perfect love casts out all fear... *1 John 4:18* (NIV)

In addition to overcoming fear, the word of God must be rooted within the heart and mind of the recipient. A word from God that exist outside of the heart and mind is a candidate for a spiritual abortion because it has no root, which is known as an ectopic pregnancy. To prevent an ectopic pregnancy, the word of God must be rooted in the heart of the recipient of God's word. This would be considered a successful implementation that helps in preventing a spiritual abortion.

**Psalms 1:1-3**
- ❖ Stay away from corrupt company.
- ❖ Keep God's word before you.
- ❖ Stand firm in God's word.
- ❖ Take root in the word.

***Colossians 2:6-8***
- ❖ Live in Christ.
- ❖ Be rooted in Christ.
- ❖ Be built in Christ.
- ❖ Be strengthened in the Faith.
- ❖ Overflow with thankfulness.
  - ➢ Overcome deception.
  - ➢ Overcome dependency of human traditions.
  - ➢ Overcome worldly standards/ principles.

So then, just as you received Christ Jesus as Lord, continue to live in him, rooted and built up in him, strengthened in the faith as you were taught, and overflowing with thankfulness. See to it that no one takes you captive through hollow and deceptive philosophy, which depends on human tradition and the basic principles of this world rather than on Christ.
**Colossians 2:6-8 (NIV)**

Hide your pregnancy until it is time to be revealed. Elizabeth was hidden for six months. Reference *Luke 1:36*

Accountability partners – individuals that hold you accountable for birthing out your vision, dreams, goals, or aspirations.

**Additional Scriptures for meditations**

- ❖ Be grounded and settled in the faith. *Colossians 1:23*
- ❖ (Be planted) Take root in the word. *Psalm 1:3, Jeremiah 17:8*
- ❖ Be planted in the Lord. *Psalm 92:13*
- ❖ Display God's splendor. *Isaiah 61:3*
- ❖ Bear Fruit. *Ezekiel 17:23-24*
- ❖ Share in the nourishing sap. *Romans 11:17-18*
- ❖ You are fitly framed. *Ephesians 2:21-22*
- ❖ Be rooted in Christ. *Ephesians 3:17- 19*
- ❖ Be filled with the fullness of God's measure. *Ephesians 3:19*
- ❖ Know what's among you. *Jude 1:12*
- ❖ Be confident in God. *Jeremiah 17:7-8*
- ❖ Discern the will of God. *Romans 12:2*

## Exercise

Read **Psalm 119:11 (NIV)** I have hidden your word in my heart that I might not sin against you.

In the scripture, Psalms 119:11, what did the psalmist say we must hide in our heart?

_____
_____
_____
_____

Why do you believe it should be hidden in our hearts?

_____

What does it mean to hide something in your heart? What takes place when something is hidden in your heart?

_____
_____
_____

What types of risks are you taking if it is not hidden in your heart?

_____
_____
_____
_____

Are there any specific assignments that God has given you that you can honestly say you have not hidden in your heart?

❏ Yes ❏ No

If so, can you name at least two?

1. _____
2. _____

What risk factors are you experiencing that are keeping you from hiding God's word in your heart?

❏ History of Spiritual Abortions ❏ People Bondage ❏ Spiritual Trauma and Infections ❏ Medications ❏ Toxic Environment ❏ Paternal Traits ❏ Spiritual Diet ❏ Self-Sabotage

Which category do you fall under in the signs of a spiritual abortion?

❏ Spiritual Disengaged ❏ Spiritual Bigamy/Adultery ❏ Spiritual Codependency

List the infections that are affecting you as it concerns the signs of a spiritual abortion.

_____   _____   _____

_____   _____   _____

How can you overcome these signs?

1. _____
   _____
   _____
   _____

2. _____
   _____
   _____
   _____

3. _____
   _____
   _____
   _____

Abortions "In The Church" Divine Strategies to Spiritual Deliverance

What methods can you use to prevent a spiritual abortion?

1. _____
2. _____
3. _____
4. _____
5. _____

Find and write down three scriptures that deal with your infectious area:

1. _____
_____
_____
_____

2. _____
_____
_____
_____

3. _____
_____
_____
_____

Meditate on scripture that deals with the area of infection. Psalms 1:3

Write down how these scriptures speak to you personally.

1. _____
_____
_____
_____

2. _____
_____
_____

3. _____
_____
_____
_____
_____
_____

Repeat this exercise for each of those areas.

Pray to the Lord concerning the areas of infection and where you first encountered this infection.

- Write down what God reveals to you concerning this area.
- If unforgiveness is discovered, forgive the person that hurt you.
- Repent for any actions that you may have done wrong (if applicable).
- Uproot the seed that was planted by renouncing and disconnecting the agreement between the pain association and the memory of your mind, heart and loins.
- Declare the word of God over your life as it concerns this area.
- Believe the word of God.
- Commit your ways unto the Lord.

Teach me, O LORD, to follow your decrees; then I will keep them to the end. **Psalm 119:33 (NIV)**

**Prayer**

Heavenly Father I come unto your throne of grace to honor you for you are Lord of lords and King of all kings. I bow down before you at your holy feet saying thank you, Lord, for being who you are Alpha and Omega the great I AM. I boldly take a stand against the accuser of the brethren as he has sought me out and devised skims to cause spiritual abortions of my purpose, dreams, visions, desires, etc. On today Father, I thank you that in the name of Jesus that every scheme and plot that the enemy has sent forth within my life are canceled. I praise you because you have declared that no weapon that has been formed shall prosper. Hallelujah!!!! Oh Lord, thank you for teaching me your ways and covering me in your truth.

I declare and decree in the name of Jesus that the hand of the adversary is loosed off my purpose, promises, dreams, visions, etc. and bind it to the pits of hell. In the name of Jesus send you consumer fire Lord and consume every spirit of associated with spiritual disengagement, adultery, and codependency that is in my life so that I will not be hindered from moving in faith. I thank you for the flames of fire consuming every lying tongue and every unclean spirit to purify my soul so we make walk upright and hope in you once again. I declare, there shall be no residue left for I am sanctified and purified through your mercy and grace by the blood of the precious lamb, our savior Jesus Christ.

I praise you, Lord, that everything that is fighting up against my prophetic destiny will fail because you are with me. In the name of Jesus, I will stand as your lamp and give birth to my purpose, visions, dreams, goals, etc. as you have established them for my life. My rock, strength, shield, and reward you are Lord. Every word you have spoken about my life shall come to pass. I'm determined to press toward the higher mark that you have called for my life. I have the mind of Christ and I am here to do your perfect will alone. I denounce my will and the will of man over my life. I will serve you, all my days. My lips shall exalt your name as you have so diligently marked out all the days of my existence.

You shall find me, Lord, in your sanctuary as I dwell in your presence. Seeking the steps that you have ordered for my life. So, that I may walk in your precepts and statutes. I come into your presence abide and take refuge because in you alone do I trust. Evil will no longer keep me from doing you will because in you I have nothing to fear. I worship you for casting out all fear and covering my multitude of sins. Your faithfulness has preserved me and kept me from death. For this, Lord, I commit my life unto you so that every word you have spoken can birth in me. I thank you that it is all done as I seal this prayer in the blood of the precious lamb who is none other than your phenomenal Son, my dynamic savior, a loving and caring friend who is none other than Jesus the Christ and it is in His Holy name that I have prayed. Amen, Amen, Amen.

## Notes & Prayer Requests

# 4

# Spiritual Stillborn

Purpose, Dreams & Vision is given to be born.

The one who received the seed that fell among the thorns is the man who hears the word, but the worries of this life and the deceitfulness of wealth choke it, making it unfruitful. *Matthew 13:22 (NIV)*

## What is a Spiritual Stillborn?

A spiritual stillborn is defined as the suffocation or death of God's word within the life of an individual due to its inability to obtain the proper nutrients for its growth and development.

## What causes a Spiritual Stillborn?

A spiritual stillborn takes place when an individual conceives the Word of God, preserves God's word, is moving and growing in the Word of God and then something takes place that stops or hinders one's growth and development. The individual has the desire to move in God's words but is bound by limitations that slowly begins to choke or kill the word because it is not being cultivated or nurtured. Whenever growth and development restrictions are present, the word of God does not have the room it needs to be cultivated within the life of the individual and cannot come to full maturity. The individual begins to choke due to suffocation, and the word eventually dies due to lack of provisions needed for its sustainment.

> If your gifts and talents are not being cultivated and utilized, then you are being setup to have a spiritual stillborn. A stillborn takes place when there is a suffocation of something until it dies. If you do not use your gifts and talents, you will lose them.

Growth restrictions cause an individual's spirit to be crushed, grieved and eventually they give up their hopes and desires of that word manifesting in its fullness. It's like a slow internal death taking place in the life of the individual as they have a desire to fulfill the word of God, but feel helpless on how to nurture it to its full maturity. Eventually a spiritual stillborn takes place because the individuals cannot see another way to provide what is needed for the growth and development of their baby. This is a very agonizing place for an individual and could be very damaging for future development.

Other numerous conditions lead an individual into having a spiritual stillborn. Conditions could include, but are not limited to selfish or inadequate leadership/mentorship, lack of training, exposure to harmful environments, lack of nourishments, different forms of abuse, no gifts and talent cultivation, the carrier's condition, cares about the world, etc.

Individuals must have the necessary substance for growth and development for the dreams, goals, desires, or aspirations in which they are carrying.

## Identifying Spiritual Stillborn High-Risk Factors

Spiritual Stillbirths carry high-risk factors that should be considered for anyone who is pregnant with a word from God. Identifying these risk factors could assist individuals in avoiding the effects of having a spiritual stillborn, as the enemy does come to choke the word from among the believer so that they cannot receive the manifestation of God's word. Here are a few risk factors that increase one's possibility of having a spiritual stillborn.

**Multiple pregnancies (Carrying multiple babies)**: An individual who is carrying more than one word (child) at the same time would be considered a very high-risk candidate for having a spiritual stillborn. Multiple pregnancies carry a very high risk to the life of the babies due to the need of being able to balance the nurturing of each child. If any child does not get the appropriate substance that he/she needs, that specific one can result in a spiritual stillborn. One who is carrying multiple babies should be very sensitive to the need of each child, so they will obtain the necessary nutrients to survive.

**Spiritual Trauma and Infections:** Individuals who receive any form of trauma or infections that is associated with limitations is at high risk for having a spiritual stillborn. Some forms of trauma that could trigger a spiritual stillborn are abuse (emotional, psychological, physical, and sexual), neglect, displacement, or restraints. These can cause an individual to withdraw, shut down and give up because of the pain associated with the event. In addition, it births disappointment, frustration, and discouragement due to the inability to properly grow due to lack of nourishment. Therefore, causing suffocation or limitation of the baby. To overcome spiritual trauma, individuals must forgive, disassociate, denounce, and/or disconnect with the agreement of the pain associated with the trauma within their heart, mind, and loins, and move in the freedom of God's word. Even if it means changing the environment(s) and kept company.

**Toxic Environment:** A toxic environment can choke the word of God out of an individual and cause them to have a spiritual stillborn. Environmental factors that will increase the likelihood of an individual having a spiritual stillborn is one that has growth limitations, the absence of proper training and development, cliquish communities, or disengaged leadership. Individuals who are experiencing any one of these environmental factors may want to consider finding environments that will provide the substance needed to bring the word of God in their life into full maturity. An environment is very important when it comes to the life of a word from God, and it makes the difference between life and death.

A word that is not cultivated cannot come to full maturity

**Paternal Traits:** Individuals cannot grow beyond the capacity of those who are providing the substance or nutrients needed for their growth and development. Growth restrictions will be placed upon the individual in the areas of their provider's limitations. Depending on the level of the word you are carrying, you may have to develop an actively engaged team of individuals who specialize in different areas, who are willing to provide you the substance needed for your growth and development. An excellent provider will also bring in and introduce you to individuals that can help you in obtaining what you are required to be sustained. *Note:* Do not leave out the Holy Spirit, because He will provide.

**Spiritual Diet:** Individuals not having the appropriate nutrients will be at high risk for having a spiritual stillborn as it breeds growth restrictions. An improper diet can cause one to be malnourished and lack substance needed for growth and development. One must have a rich diet that is suitable for what he or she is carrying in order to sustain from conception to completion. If your diet does not consist of what you need to grow and develop, then you should become proactive in finding a source that provides the required nutrients. Outside of your personal relationship with God, a healthy spiritual diet could include educational opportunities, mentorship, small groups, etc.

Jesus answered, "It is written: 'Man does not live on bread alone, but on every word that comes from the mouth of God.'"
**Matthew 4:4 (NIV)**

## Spiritual Stillborn Warning Signs

Often believers find themselves in environments where the ground is fallow, and it's difficult to birth due to growth restrictions. They may consist of lack of nourishments, unfruitfulness, stress, etc. One must be very sensitive to their environment and their company as it concerns the need for the growth and development of their baby. Lack of sensitivity has caused many visions, dreams, and desires to die. There are many warning signs to evaluate that chokes or suffocates the life out of a fetus. We will examine warning signs associated with a spiritual stillborn.

**Spiritual Pharaoh**: A spiritual Pharaoh is an individual, environment or substance that oppress, depress, and suppress an individual physically, emotionally, psychologically, and/or financially through the suffocation of one's needs to grow and develop. In the book of Exodus chapter 1, the children of Israel found themselves under a spiritual Pharaoh who devised a plan to oppress them to keep them from growing. His plan consisted of harsh and brutal treatment of the Israelites and the death of their sons at childbirth.

To break free from a spiritual Pharaoh, an individual must understand the truth of God, pray without ceasing, not be moved by their conditions or environment, not compromise God's word and move in the instruction of God. One must come out from under the spirit of Pharaoh to birth out God's word. Exodus 3:7-10

Every word must have the proper nutrient so that it may grow into maturity.

**Infections:** fear, oppression, burden, pain, affliction, bitter, depression, enslavement, persecution, hard labor, premature death, suffocation, frustration, deception, murder, discouragement, suffering, man-pleasing, codependency, lack of trust, etc.

**Ways to overcome spiritual Pharaoh.**

- ❖ Remember the promises of God. ***Psalm 103:1-2, Lamentations 3:21***
- ❖ Trust God. Psalm 37:3
- ❖ Cry out to God. ***Exodus 2:23-25***
- ❖ Don't shrink back. ***Hebrews 10:38-39***
- ❖ Don't allow others to affect your growth. ***Galatians 5:7-10***
- ❖ Be obedient unto the Lord. ***1 Peter 1:14***
- ❖ Be faithful. ***Matthew 25:23***
- ❖ Don't get bitter. ***Hebrews 12:15***
- ❖ Press toward the mark. ***Philippians 3:14***
- ❖ Remember that He heals hearts and wounds. ***Psalm 147***

Spiritual Stillborn

## *Prenatal Visit*

**Scripture Study:** Read Genesis 16 & 21:9-21        **Person:** Hagar

**Assignment**

Can you diagnose who is the responsible individual(s) for Hagar's potential spiritual stillborn?
_____

Give us the diagnosis report of the high-risk factors that make Hagar a possible candidate for a spiritual stillborn?

- ❏ Spiritual Maturity
- ❏ History of Spiritual Miscarriages
- ❏ Spiritual Dysfunctions
- ❏ Spiritual Trauma and Infections
- ❏ Medications
- ❏ Paternal Traits
- ❏ Toxic Environment
- ❏ Spiritual Diet
- ❏ _____

Can you provide us with a list of infections that contribute to Hagar's potential spiritual stillborn?

_____    _____    _____
_____    _____    _____


What can you take away from this experience that would assist you in escaping a spiritually pharaoh in your personal life?
_____
_____
_____
_____
_____

**Spiritual blindness:** Spiritual blindness is the inability to see the will of God due to lack of perception, awareness, judgment, ignorance, etc. It limits an individual's ability to see or perceive the truth due to several forms of deception and manipulation. There are several conditions that cause spiritual blindness within the life of individuals. They include, but are not limited to, blind leaders, lack of understanding, confidence in man, the love of darkness, hardened hearts, deaf ears, blinded minds, rejection of truth, etc. It has caused many spiritual stillbirths in the life of the children of God. The largest recorded stillbirths due to spiritual blindness are in the book of numbers chapter 13 & 14 when the spies came and gave their report about the land of Canaan. Due to the report of ten spiritually blinded leaders all of Israel whom originally left Egypt except for Joshua and Caleb did not enter the promise land because they believed and was led by the spiritually blinded. Israel's thoughts about the report begin to suffocate their belief and it caused them give up on entering the promises land. Their minds begin to become bombard with thoughts such as "if they only would have died in Egypt or the wilderness, their wives and children will be taken for plunder, the Lord brought them to the promise land so they could fall by the sword" and this prompt them to want to go back to Egypt, to even chose their own leader to take them back and to desire to stone their current leaders. The dwelling of these thoughts caused Israel to become spiritually blinded with disbelief among them and they chose to forfeit entering the promise land. This was a

So, I tell you this, and insist on it in the Lord, that you must no longer live as the Gentiles do, in the futility of their thinking. They are darkened in their understanding and separated from the life of God because of the ignorance that is in them due to the hardening of their hearts. Having lost all sensitivity, they have given themselves over to sensuality so as to indulge in every kind of impurity, with a continual lust for more.

*Ephesians 4:17-19 (NIV) –*

major tragedy for Israel as they were close to entering the promised land, but did not obtain the promise. Note that as you read the story, God held everyone responsible for their own belief or actions. Therefore, one cannot blame their blindness, ignorance or wrong decision on someone else.

**Infections:** fear, rejection, low self-esteem, insecurities, lack of confidence, temptation, loneliness, worry, depression, persecution, ignorance, harden heart, tradition, religion, rebellion, greed, procrastination, disbelief, lack of personal relationship, double-mindedness, etc.

**Ways to overcome spiritual blindness.**

- Follow Christ. *John 8:12*
- Build your faith. *Romans 10:17, Jude 1:20*
- Open your eyes. *Luke 24:31*
- See the vision of God. *Numbers 24:4*
- Hear the word of God. *Luke 11:28*
- Take personal accountability. *1 Chronicles 21:16-17*
- Take away the veil. *2 Corinthians 3:16*
- Let your heart be enlightened. *Ephesians 1:18*
- Walk as a child of light. *Ephesians 5:8*
- Pray for God to open your eyes. *Matthew 20:33, 2 Kings 6:17*
- Regain your sight. *Mark 10:51*
- Remove from the darkness. *Acts 9:40*
- Receive the forgiveness of sins. *Acts 26:18*
- Repent. *Acts 3:19*
- Gain understanding. *Proverbs 23:23*
- Connect with those who give you sight to give your baby life. *2 Kings 4:32-37*
- Be established in God's word. *1 Chronicles 14:2*

Abortions "In The Church" Divine Strategies to Spiritual Deliverance

## *Prenatal Visit*

**Scripture Study:** Read numbers 13 & 14       **Person:** 10 spies

**Assignment**

Looking at Isreal's History, would you consider them to be at high-risk of having a spiritual stillborn? ❑ Yes ❑No

Why or Why not?

_____
_____
_____

Provide us with the diagnosed high-risk factors that contributed to this spiritual stillborn.

❑ Spiritual Maturity                   ❑ Medications
❑ History of Spiritual Miscarriages    ❑ Paternal Traits
❑ Spiritual Dysfunctions               ❑ Toxic Environment
❑ Spiritual Trauma and Infections      ❑ Spiritual Diet
❑ _____

What areas of infections can you identify that leads to the diagnoses of a spiritual abortion?

_____   _____   _____
_____   _____   _____

What can you take away from this experience that would assist you in not being spiritually blind in your personal life?

_____
_____
_____
_____
_____

**Spiritual Idolatry**: Spiritual Idolatry is the worship, servitude, and homage paid to people, places or things, rather than to God. It causes individuals to esteem people, things and situations above God and His word, which leads to the delivery of a spiritual stillborn. Spiritual idolatry is an offense against God and can be considered as high treason as it hinders individuals from moving in their purpose and obtaining the promises of God. When the Israelites were given instruction on the possession of the land, they were commanded to destroy all traces of the existing idolatry of the Canaanites because any form of idol worshiping would be detestable to the Lord. Idol worshiping keeps individuals distracted from birthing out the word of God. Many people are in jobs, relationships, religious institutions, or under leadership that are hindering them from developing and growing in their God-given purpose. The same fate is upon those whose possession such as money, cars, social status, or power, has become their God.

Throughout history, man has set up idols that have hindered them from moving in the things of God. Read Joshua 7 and see how Achan caused Israel to be defeated by their enemies due to spiritual idolatry. Israel was supposed to deliver a victory against their enemies but because of Achan actions they had a stillborn and victory was dead unto them. Individuals must devote their hearts to God, remove their foreign gods, and serve God alone to be delivered from having a spiritual stillborn due to spiritual idolatry.

**Infections:** witchcraft, blurred vision, fear, distraction, rebellious, unfaithfulness, covetousness, greed, prostitution, adultery, pride, arrogance, rejection, impurity, lust, evil desire, sexual immorality, faithless, deception, addictions, etc.

**Ways to overcome spiritual idolatry.**

- ❖ Fear the Lord. *Joshua 24:14-15*
- ❖ Don't turn aside from God's word. *Joshua 23:6-7, Deuteronomy 18:14*
- ❖ Burn up and destroy idols. *Deuteronomy 7:5*

- ❖ Don't hold on to the tradition of man. ***Mark 7:8-9***
- ❖ Do not make a covenant with others and their gods. ***Exodus 23:32***
- ❖ Do not bow down to Baal. ***Psalm 81:9-10***
- ❖ Break down every altar and high place. ***Exodus 34:13***
- ❖ Destroy all places of idol worship. ***Deuteronomy 12:1-3***
- ❖ Keep yourself from idols. ***1 John 5:21***
- ❖ Flee from idolatry. ***1 Corinthians 10:14***
- ❖ Acknowledge no other gods. ***Hosea 13:4***
- ❖ Put idolatry to death. ***Colossians 3:5***
- ❖ Be devoted to God above everything. ***Deuteronomy 4:23***
- ❖ Devote your heart to God. ***Joshua 24:14***
- ❖ Look to God for your security. ***Judges 10:13-16***
- ❖ Don't forget God. ***Psalm 106:19-22***
- ❖ Choose to serve God. ***Luke 16:13***

## *Prenatal Visit*

**Scripture Study:** Read Joshua 7:1-8:2    **Person:** Achan & Israel

**Assignment**

Can you identify any known high-risk factors that could potentially cause Israel to have a spiritual stillborn? ❏ Yes ❏ No

If so, provide us with the diagnosed high-risk factors that could contribute to Israel having a spiritual stillborn

❏ Spiritual Maturity
❏ History of Spiritual Miscarriages
❏ Spiritual Dysfunctions
❏ Spiritual Trauma and Infections
❏ _____

❏ Medications
❏ Paternal Traits
❏ Toxic Environment
❏ Spiritual Diet

Provide evidence of your diagnoses
_____
_____
_____
_____

What areas of infections can you diagnose in Achans behavior that indicate the Israelites would have a spiritual stillborn?

_____    _____    _____
_____    _____    _____

How did Israel cancel any further spiritual stillbirths under Achans behavior?
_____
_____
_____
_____

## Prevention Methods for Spiritual Stillbirths

Spiritual Stillbirths are very common in the church due to various factors in the life of believers. However, there are preventative methods that could assist believers from having a spiritual stillborn. Paul gives some very simple and plain strategies as he talks to the believer in Philippians 3:12-15. These strategies can be very useful and vital in aiding those who are facing a spiritual stillborn. He said, don't consider oneself as perfect, press on to take hold of your assignment, forgetting those things which are behind you, straining for what ahead, and press on toward the goal to win the prize for which God has called you.

What I love about the Apostle Paul in the text, he used the personal pronoun I. In so, many words he declared that he was taking personal responsibility and accountability for his calling despite what he was going through. He chose not to allow anything or anybody to hinder him from moving forward in his assignment. Let's review what Paul is saying to assist in spiritual stillbirth prevention.

- ❖ **Don't be a perfectionist.** Paul is saying, that he has not obtained everything, and he is not perfect, but he is not going to allow that to stop him from moving forward in his assignment.

"Before she goes into labor, she gives birth; before the pains come upon her, she delivers a son. Who has ever heard of such a thing? Who has ever seen such things? Can a country be born in a day or a nation be brought forth in a moment? Yet no sooner is Zion in labor than she gives birth to her children. says your God.

**Isaiah 66:9 (NIV}**

Perfection is my aim not who I am. Attempting to be a perfectionist can cause a spiritual stillborn in the life of believers as it hinders individuals from birthing because they are always looking for everything to be absolutely perfect. Perfectionist operates with delay, deterrence, and procrastination. Christ has taken hold of us to perfect us, and when we come perfected, then our race has been completed.

- ❖ **Press on in your assignment.** Paul is stating, "Advance in your assignment so that perfection can be complete in you." Be confident that He who started a good work in you shall complete it to the very end. To not advance in your purpose is to give up, producing a spiritual stillborn. We must decide that we are going to pursue what God has given unto us no matter what. The press says that something is up against what you are doing. So, it's going to take some effort on your part to achieve the task.

- ❖ **Forget and Forgive the past.** Holding on to the past can cause an individual to become stuck and stagnated and produce a spiritual stillborn. Pulling the past of hurt, shame, discouragement, or disappointment will only weigh you down, keep you distracted, constrained and unproductive. It's like the umbilical cord being wrapped around the baby's neck depriving its oxygen to live. Forgetting and forgiving those things that are behind you are vital to moving forward as it sets you free to move with liberty and no constraints.

- ❖ **Stretch your capacity.** Paul talks about straining or reaching for what's ahead, meaning that one must stretch himself to obtain what's ahead of them. Our capacity must stretch us to dwell in the place in which God is calling us. We cannot be in a place of complacency in our purpose as it will cause a spiritual stillborn. Complacency hinders capacity so we must be willing to extend ourselves beyond our current limitations. Babies always need room to grow and stretch.

- ❖ **Make the Mark.** We must take personal accountability and responsibility for the assignment that God has given unto us. If we fail to do so, we will repetitiously have a spiritual stillborn. Too often, we placed a dependency on others to deliver or move in our assignment from God. This has led many with incomplete assignments. We must move by faith in what God has given unto us even if we must do it all by ourselves. Believers must cultivate a faith that totally depends on God so that we can win the prize. To make the mark, we must become focused on the goal that is ahead, according to the call that God has marked out for us. It involves being authentic to yourself and your calling. Authenticity gives you the fuel to press on toward the goal to win the prize for which God has called you.

**Additional Scriptures**
- ❖ Know that all things work together. **Romans. 8:28**
- ❖ Run to win the prize. **1 Corinthians 9:24**
- ❖ Put no confidence in the flesh. **Philippians 3:3**
- ❖ Set your mind on Jesus. **Hebrews 3:1**
- ❖ Move to maturity in Christ Jesus. **Hebrews 6:1**
- ❖ Fight the good fight of faith. **2 Timothy 4:7-8**
- ❖ Overcome by the blood of the lamb. **Revelation**
- ➢ Do not be bewitched. **Galatians 3:1**
- ❖ Don't let anyone disqualify you. **Colossians 2:18-19**
- ❖ Persevere under trials. **James 1:1**
- ❖ Run with endurance. **Hebrews 12:1**
- ❖ Obey the truth. **Galatians 5:7**
- ❖ Discipline your body. **1 Corinthians 9:27**
- ❖ Faint not, you shall reap the harvest. **Galatians 6:9**
- ❖ Gird up the loins of your mind. **1 Peter 1:13**
- ❖ Go on unto perfection. **Hebrews 6:1**

## Exercise

**Read: John 15: 4**

Remain in me, and I will remain in you. No branch can bear fruit by itself; it must remain in the vine. Neither can you bear fruit unless you remain in me. *John 15:4 (NIV)*

In the scripture, John 15: 4, what did Jesus say we must do?
_____
_____

Define the word remain in your own words within the context of John 15:4.
_____
_____
_____

List five synonyms that that means the same as remain
_____
_____

What types of risks are you taking for not remaining in Christ with your purpose, goals, dreams, vision, etc?
_____
_____

How can abiding in Christ prevent you from having a spiritual stillborn?
_____
_____
_____

**Review Psalm 37:5** as it takes personal commitment to main in Christ Jesus. How does this scripture personally speak to you?

_____
_____
_____

Are there any specific assignments that God has given you that you can honestly say you have not committed unto the Lord?
❏ Yes ❏ No
If so, can you name at least two?

1. _____
2. _____

What risk factors are you experiencing that are keeping you from remaining in Jesus Christ?

❏ History of Spiritual Abortions ❏ People Bondage
❏ Medications ❏ Toxic Environment ❏ Paternal Traits
❏ Spiritual Diet ❏ Self-Sabotage
❏ Spiritual Trauma and Infections

What warning signs are you experiencing that could indicate that you are in jeopardy of having a spiritual stillborn?
❏ Spiritual Pharaoh ❏ Spiritual Blindness ❏ Spiritual Idolatry

What infectious areas can you identify that has caused you not to commit these areas unto the Lord.

_____    _____    _____

_____    _____    _____

Identify three ways you overcome these signs?

1. _____
   _____
   _____
   _____
   _____

2. _____
   _____
   _____
   _____
   _____

3. _____
   _____
   _____
   _____
   _____

What methods can you use to prevent a spiritual stillborn?

1. _____
2. _____
3. _____
4. _____
5. _____

Find and write down three scriptures that deal with your infectious area:

1. _____
   _____
   _____

2. _____
   _____
   _____

3. _____
   _____
   _____

Meditate on scripture that deals with the area of infection.
Write down how these scriptures speak to you personally.

1. _____
   _____
   _____

2. _____
   _____
   _____

3. _____
   _____
   _____

**Prayer**

Oh, precious Lord, I come into your Holy presence in reverence of who you are in my life. My Heavenly Father, my Strong tower, My Provisionary, my Healer, my everything. Master., my arms are stretch out before you as I surrender it all unto you. I lay every matter, every weight, every heartbreak, every disappointment, etc before you that has been a hindrance in me birthing out your word of truth. I know that you care for me Father and it is your desire to perfect everything concerning me.

With Kingdom boldness, In the name of Jesus, I ask that my eyes of my heart be enlightened in order that I may know the hope to which You have called me, in the riches of Your glorious inheritance and Your incomparably great power for me as it is written in Ephesians 1:18-19. I asked with a repentance heart that my faith is restored in you. Things have happened, in my lift that has shifted me like wheat and caused me to have spiritual stillbirths with my purpose, visions, goals, dreams, etc. Help me our Lord and deliver me from every wound that I have acquired from the spiritual pharaoh's, spiritual blindness and spiritual idolatry in the name of Jesus. I repent unto you Lord, for denying your power to work in my life. Restore me, Oh Lord. It's by faith alone that I will give birth to your word as it is the evidence of the things in which I hope. Father my faith is what engages and activated my confidence in you. I chose to contend for my faith and fight the good fight of faith in the name of Jesus.

I magnify your name Father for contending with those things that have been contending with me. I recognize if you before me who can stand against me. So, I prevail over every work of the enemy, every hindrance, giant, stumbling block and mountain that has been sent to cause me to have a spiritual stillborn of your word. In the name of Jesus, I serve an eviction notice to the enemy in my mind, in my heart, in my territory that has been trying to suffocate my purpose, visions, goals, dreams, etc. You said, if I decree a thing, it shall be established. So, I declare and decree in the name of Jesus that my enemies shall scatter. They shall fall before me and not touch the tents of my dwelling. Every wall that the enemy has erected to cause spiritual stillbirths in my life I demolish in the name of Jesus. I tear down every strong tower and high place of the enemy in my life, in the name of Jesus. Every idol in my life, I destroy by the fire of the Holy Ghost. The tent of my dwelling shall enlarge and I move forward in your word for my life. I shall not be confined any longer by the deception, accusations, and hurt caused by the enemy. I declare that peoples, places or things will no longer keep me back from moving in my destiny. I shall move in the steps that you have ordered from my life without delay, procrastination, and hesitation in the majestic name of Jesus. My purpose, promises, dreams, visions, etc. shall spring forth like the river of living water.

I stand in what you have called forth in my life as the Garden of Eden where rivers of prosperity flow consistently into my life. They shall not dry up as I move the plans that you have declared for my life. I shall never again be without understanding and wisdom of your word coming to life in me. I shall perceive everything you are doing in my life as I hide your word in my heart.

You said in your word that you shall not call me to the point of delivery and shut up my womb and I trust you at your words. I shall walk in my purpose. I shall birth my dreams, goals, visions, aspirations, etc. in Jesus. I bless your name, Father. I cover and seal this prayer in the blood of Jesus. I declare that no one of them will fall to the ground and it's in the majestic name of Jesus, I pray. Amen, Amen, Amen.

Do I bring to the moment of birth and not give delivery?" says the LORD. "Do I close up the womb when I bring to delivery?" says your God.

**Isaiah 66:9 (NIV)**

## Notes & Prayer Requests

# Work Book Sample

Abortions "In The Church
Divine Strategies to Spiritual Deliverance
Workbook

**Coming Soon!!!!**

Abortions "In The Church" Divine Strategies to Spiritual Deliverance

```
┌─────────────────────────────┐
│       Patient Chart         │
│         Jeroboam            │
└─────────────────────────────┘
```

**Scripture Study:** 1 Kings 11:26-14:20.

**Vital Statistics:**
- Where: The northern kingdom of Israel
- Occupations: Project foreman, king of Israel
- Relatives: Father: Nebat. Mother: Zeruah. Sons: Abijah, Nadab.
- Contemporaries: Solomon, Nathan, Ahijah, Rehoboam

**Immunizations:**
- An effective leader and organizer
- First king of the 10 tribes of Israel in the divided kingdom
- A charismatic leader with much popular support

**Infections/Diseases/ Allergies:**
- Erected idols in Israel to keep people away from the Temple in Jerusalem
- Appointed priests from outside the tribe of Levi
- Depended more on his own cunning than on God's promises

**Physical History:**
- Great opportunities are often destroyed by small decisions
- Careless efforts to correct another's errors often lead to the same errors
- Mistakes always occur when we attempt to take over God's role in a situation

**Lab work: Ordered Test:**
- To rule over the 10 northern tribes of Israel
- Follow God's command,
- Walk in God's ways,
- Do right in the eyes of God by keeping His statutes and commands,
- Follow the pattern of King David

**Confidential Patient Notes:**

Jeroboam was a man who had good leadership skills that were recognized by King Solomon and God. When King Solomon attitude changed toward God as a consequence God took 10 of the tribes of Israel out of his hands. The person who God had chosen to take this prestige position was Jeroboam. He became the 1st King to rule over the 10 tribes of Israel. God gave him the following commands. *"And if you will listen to all that I command you, and will walk in my ways, and do what is right in my eyes by keeping my statutes and my commandments, as David my servant did, I will be with you and will build you a sure house, as I built for David, and I will give Israel to you.* **1 Kings 11:38 (ESV)".** At this time, Jeroboam was not able to obtain the kingdom because he had to wait until King Solomon death. After the king's death and the right conditions, Jeroboam was handed the 10 tribes as promised by God.

When King Jeroboam got into position he received some negative thought and it put fear in the heart of the newly establish king. Then he turned some very unwise counselor who could not have known the commandments of the Lord or the history of Israel. Because their actions lead them to repeat Israel history and breaking the Ten Commandments. This fear caused the king to do the opposite of what the Lord had instructed him to do. Therefore, it caused him to have a spiritual miscarriage that led to the following consequences: reference: **1 Kings 14:10-16**

*Lab Work Results:*
- Jeroboam kingdom would be destroyed
- Dishonorable death to every male (free or slave) under Jeroboam. With the exception of the sick son.
- The wife had to carry the burden of the bad news
- The Lord would raise up a king to kill Jeroboam entire family.
- The entire nation of Israel would be struck down, uprooted, scattered, and sent into exile because they followed Jeroboam leadership and participated in false worship and idolatry.
- The removal of God's hands upon Israel because they followed his sin.

# Abortions "In The Church" Divine Strategies to Spiritual Deliverance

## *Prenatal Diagnoses*

1. Was Jeroboam a likely candidate for a spiritual miscarriage?
   ❑ Yes ❑No

2. Can Jeroboam be diagnosed with any high-risk factor(s) that can potentially make Jeroboam a candidate for a spiritual miscarriage?

   ❑ Spiritual Maturity          ❑ Paternal Traits
   ❑ Spiritual Dysfunctions      ❑ Spiritual Diet
   ❑ Spiritual Trauma and Infections  ❑ Medications
   ❑ History of Spiritual Miscarriages ❑ Toxin Environment
   ❑ _____

3. If, so can you explain your diagnoses
   _____
   _____
   _____
   _____
   _____

4. Based upon Jeroboam chart can you identify signs of a potential spiritual miscarriage? ❑ Yes ❑No

5. If so, what were the signs?
   ❑ Spiritual Ignorance      ❑ Spiritual Bleeding
   ❑ Spiritual Torment

6. Chart the areas of infections that are warning signs for Jeroboam's spiritual miscarriage

   _____        _____
   _____        _____
   _____        _____
   _____        _____
   _____

Chart the diagnoses of Jeroboam spiritual miscarriage.

_____
_____
_____
_____
_____

**Prenatal Aftercare Treatment**

Can you provide Jeroboam with medical advice after care that would assist him from having a future spiritual miscarriage?

_____
_____
_____
_____
_____
_____
_____
_____

**Prescription Scripture (s)**

_____
_____
_____
_____
_____
_____

**Look out for other titles**

The Birthing Process

Spiritual Midwife Training Manual

Preserving Destiny through the Power of Prayer: A Spiritual Warfare Prayer Collection

Rules of Success: Investment 101

## Authors Bio

**Kingdom Strategist**, Blueprint Builder, and Spiritual Midwife **Pastor Derashay Zorn** is an international mentor and expert on the art of **unleashing purpose, developing dreams, and expanding untapped potentials within individuals, corporations, and ministries.** Her passion for information technology led her to obtain a Master of Science in Information System Management, which equipped her to specialize in analyzing, developing and managing systems to birth or expand individuals and entities into the next dimension of kingdom implementation.

Mrs. Zorn has been an intricate part of community collaborations through bridging the gap between community entities. Derashay believes in building stronger communities through encouraging, empowering, and educating families. Mrs. Zorn has held various leadership positions within the community and has done extensive work in nonprofit organizations. Derashay has been involved in, but not limited to, nonprofit startups, technology analysis and implementation, online education platform design, implementation, and development, as well as establishing curriculums and training programs. In addition to being a wife and mother of three amazing sons, she is a pastor, entrepreneur, consultant, empowerment speaker, mentor, and friend.

As an overcomer of a chaotic life to an extraordinary life, Pastor Derashay has been given firsthand experience on how a life of principles can rearrange and position one's life to fulfill purpose. Her ability to overcome through the application of God's word has been the birthing grounds for Divine Order Restoration Ministries (D.O.R.M.) International where God has mandated her to "Restore the Order of God One Life, One Body, and One Nation at a Time." For such a time as this God has sent her forth to release Kingdom Strategies that will empower, educate, equip and employ individuals into great dimension within their destinies.

Pastor Derashay equips mankind globally as the founder and host of the weekly "**In The Church**" **TV/Radio Broadcast** where they are shining the light of God's word "In the Church" to discuss and resolve real everyday issues that are taking place around the world exposes the good, the bad and the ugly. Mrs. Zorn's heart for women led her to equip them globally through her FREE digital *Women of Influence Magazine publication*. Under her leadership, she has implemented several educational biblical platforms to develop individuals daily within their purpose and prayer initiatives, such as the 365/24/7 International Prayer Call Center to motivate and encourage God's people.

Now, through **Kingdom Strategies University**® and her **School of Vision Bootcamp**, she teaches others **how to maximize their potential and monetize their gifts and talents** as a critical vehicle of fulfilling purpose, making significant impacts and branding influence that can instantly and beautifully change the world.

Her philosophy is **"A critical tool to self-development is learning how to cultivate, build and release others into their destinies.**

**Contact information**

**Email Address:**
dzorn@divine-order.org
dzorn@inthechurch.com
dz@derashayzorn.com

**Website**:
| **Ministry** | **Business** |
| --- | --- |
| www.divine-order.org | www.derashayzorn.com |
| www.inthechurch.com | |

**Social media**:
| **Ministry** | **Business** |
| --- | --- |
| **Twitter:** inthechurchlive | kbstrategist |
| **Facebook:** inthechurch | kingdombusinessstrategist |
| **Instagram:** inthechurch | kingdomstrategist |

**Make The Pledge** - Make the pledge to give birth to your purpose, dreams, visions, goals, desires, etc. Obtain your Delivering Greatness commitment seal. Join the Birthing Chambers FB group and be a part of a nurturing environment/community for giving birth and expanding in your purpose.

**Purchase The Book**: Obtain a few copies of the book and be a blessing to a few people. Go to www.inthechurch.com

**Book Me:** Book me as your keynote speaker, workshop facilitator, motivational speaker, intercessor at your next event. www.derashayzorn.com

**Host a Campaign Event** (retreat, conference, seminar, summit, etc): Host an event that is centered around birthing out purpose, dreams, visions, goals, etc. and include us in the party

**Join a Campaign Event:** Watch out for our upcoming local, state, national or international events, register and get engaged in the movement. Watch out for the Summer & Winter Conference, Fall Birthing Chambers Retreat and a host of webinars.

**Sponsor a Campaign Event:** Become a sponsor by participating in events sponsorship opportunities.

**Share The Campaign:** Share the campaign information with others you know that could benefit from joining the movement

### Conference / Summit/Seminar/Speaking Empowerment Topics and Training

I'm Pregnant with Possibilities
Delivering my Expectations
Planned Pregnancy
I Think I'm pregnant
Overcoming/Avoiding the Pitfalls of having a spiritual miscarriage, abortion & stillborn
Avoiding SIDS
False Labor Pain
Avoiding Premature Birth
Resuscitate my baby
Balancing my pregnancy
How to deliver a healthy baby
Trusting others with you baby
My baby need to grow up
It takes a village to raise this baby
My Baby Just L.E.A.P
Kingdom Business: Non-Negotiable
B.O.S.S. (Birthing Out Successful Solutions) Business Strategy Series
F Factors (Fear. Faith. Favor)

**Customized programs or topics upon request**

.

**Abortions in the Church –** *Divine Strategies to Spiritual Deliverance* is a book designed to spring forth a spiritual awakening in the church across the world as it brings deliverance unto Gods people. It speaks to the body of Christ about the bloodshed that is taken place in God's house day after day and assembly after assembly, as it sheds light on the spiritual miscarriages, abortions, and stillbirths that are taking place right in the church of God's promises, visions, dreams, and purposes for His people. While exposing its direct connection to the murders and deaths that are taking place naturally, the bloodshed must end on the inside of the church before it reaches beyond its walls. Abortions in the Church – *Divine Strategies to Spiritual Deliverance* provides strategies on how to be delivered from those things that cause spiritual miscarriages, abortions, and stillbirths so that one can deliver the manifestation of God's word within their lives.

With these strategies, you can
- Understand what a spiritual abortion, miscarriage and stillborn entails
- Recognize the risk factors and signs of having a spiritual abortion, miscarriage and stillborn
- Obtain preventive methods to eliminate spiritual abortions, miscarriages, and stillbirths
- Identify areas that has caused or could cause interruption in your purpose, goals, visions, dreams, desires or mission.
- Conceive and preserve the word of God
- Overcome opposition that has hindered you from living out your purpose, living your dreams, goals, visions, aspirations, etc.

www.ingramcontent.com/pod-product-compliance
Lightning Source LLC
LaVergne TN
LVHW051507070426
835507LV00022B/2974